This book is a gift to: _____

_____

From: _____

Date: _____

Words of Love

© 2011   Christian Art Gifts, RSA
          Christian Art Gifts Inc., IL, USA

Designed by Christian Art Gifts

Images used under license from Shutterstock.com

Scripture quotations are taken from the *Holy Bible*, New Living Translation®, second edition. Copyright © 1996, 2004, 2007 by Tyndale House Publishers, Inc., Carol Stream, Illinois 60188. All rights reserved.

Printed in China

ISBN 978-1-77036-938-2

11 12 13 14 15 16 17 18 19 20 – 10 9 8 7 6 5 4 3 2 1

christian
art gifts.

Our Lord does not care so much for the importance of our works as for the love with which they are done.

Teresa of Avila

Love is something

more stern and **splendid**

than mere kindness.

C. S. Lewis

Love is a fabric

which **never fades**, no matter

how often it is washed

in the waters of adversity and grief.

Anonymous

Praise the Lord

because He is good to us,

and His love
never fails.

Love attempts
what is above its

STRENGTH.

Thomas à Kempis

Love all of God's creation,

the whole of it and every grain of sand in it.

Love every leaf, every ray of God's light.

Love the animals, love the plants,

love everything.

If you love everything, you will perceive

the divine mystery in things.

Once you have perceived it, you will begin to

comprehend it better every day,

and you will come at last to love the world

with an **all-embracing love.**

Fyodor Dostoyevski

God loves
and cares
for each one
of us as if
there were only
one of us.

Augustine of Hippo

15

Joy is love enjoying.

Peace is love resting.

Patience is love waiting.

Kindness is love reacting.

Goodness is love choosing.

Faithfulness is love keeping its word.

Gentleness is love empathizing.

Self-control is love in charge.

Charles Stanley

My soul
is satisfied
to know
His love
can never fail.

E. S. Hall

Love covers over all wrongs.

Prov. 10:12

Love can never more grow old,

Locks may lose their brown and gold,

Cheeks may fade and hollow grow,

But the hearts that love will know,

Never winter's frost and chill,

Summer's warmth is in them still.

Eben Eugene Rexford

There are many who want me to tell

them of secret ways of becoming perfect

and I can only tell them that the sole secret

is a hearty love of God,

and the only way of attaining that

love is by loving.

You learn to speak by speaking,

to study by studying, to run by running,

to work by working;

and just so you learn to love God

and man by loving.

Francis of Sales

God bless everybody I love;

God bless everybody who loves me;

God bless everybody

who loves everybody who I love,

And everybody

who loves everybody who loves me.

A Colonial Child's Prayer

To love is to find pleasure

in the happiness of the person loved.

Baron Gottfried Wilhelm von Leibnitz

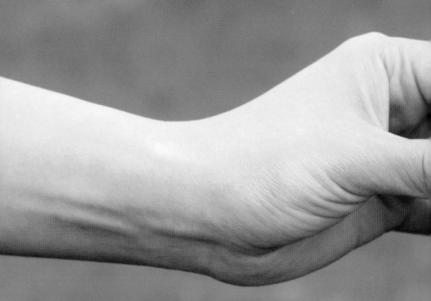

Spread
love
everywhere
you go.

Mother Teresa

One who loves is borne on wings;

he runs, and is

filled with joy;

he is **free** and unrestricted.

He gives all to receive all,

and he has all in all;

for beyond all things he **rests**

in the one highest thing,

from whom streams all that is good.

Thomas à Kempis

Love

comforteth like

sunshine

after rain.

William Shakespeare

If God cares

so **wonderfully**

for flowers

that are here today

and thrown into the fire tomorrow,

He will certainly

care for you.

Luke 12:28

It is difficult to know

at what moment love begins;

it is less difficult to know

that it has begun.

Henry Wadsworth Longfellow

The love

we give away

is the only love

we keep.

Elbert Hubbard

Love is patient and kind. 1 Cor. 13:4

God sends each person

into this world with a

special message

to deliver, with a

special song to sing,

with a special act

of love to bestow.

John Powell

Let us continue

to love one another,

for love

comes from God.

1 John 4:7

And now these three remain:

faith,
hope
and love.

But the greatest of these is love.

1 Cor. 13:13